Village Voices

A celebration of poetry and art from the South Pennines

Maytree Press 2023

Published 2023 by Maytree Press

www.maytreepress.co.uk

ISBN: 978-1-913508-33-3

A CIP catalogue record of this book is available from the
British Library.

Cover image: *Buildings of Marsden, Huddersfield* © Ashley Cundall

Maytree 043

Contents:

Titles of artworks are shown in *Italics*.
An alphabetical list of all the poems can be found at the end of the book..

ART REPRESENTING COMMUNITY

Painting is silent poetry, and poetry is painting that speaks.
Plutarch, Greek Philosopher 46-120 AD

Foreword

Marsden, the Poetry Village

Marsden is a village in the South Pennines with a rich poetry heritage. It was the birthplace of dialect poet Samuel Laycock (1826-1893) and more recently the current Poet Laureate, Simon Armitage. It has a strong tradition of poetry readings: in the Marsden Mechanics building, in the streets, in pubs and on organised walks. Poems can often be found in shop windows, and even carved into rocks – the so-called *Stanza Stones*.

"Village Voices" was initiated by the very active group, Marsden Community Poetry. It has been my privilege to run the Open Mic events for them since June 2022. It was at one such meeting where discussion turned to the difficulty many excellent poets faced in getting their work published. We decided upon a project to publish an anthology of poems from all sections of the community. It sounded like an exciting challenge, so I decided to run with it. I had no idea what I was letting myself in for.

Producing this anthology has been a roller-coaster ride, and a lot of work, but ultimately very rewarding. I have met many poets and artists during the process and made connections with several other poetry groups.

Contributors are located throughout the South Pennines and beyond. They were invited to submit several poems from which one would be chosen, thus enabling the anthology both to be inclusive and to achieve a high standard of work.

Art is positioned throughout, to enrich and diversify the readers' experience.

In keeping with its poetry traditions, Marsden is home to a successful poetry publisher, Maytree Press, who have a large portfolio of accomplished poets. We are privileged that they have published this book.

Appreciation of both poetry and art is very personal and subjective so the wide variety achieved in "Village Voices" will fill your soul with inspiration, enjoyment, and a connection with the local community.

Kathy Trout
Chair, Marsden Community Poetry

Poetry is

A concert hall
where music underscoring memory,
echoes sense and, moves the mind of many
as it sings through separate salons
to the rhythm of one heart;
a picture
framing the event,
offering a point of view,
image artfully arranged,
in which tone and tint
drip hints and shades of meaning;
a party
where the host cries, 'come in and
share my private dream home,
climb the stairs to my brain,
forage in the stanza of my heart
and help yourself to anything I fancy
before you close the door and part';
a mirror
offering up reflection,
from which glassy depths
surface, polished into words,
what we always knew
and intimately recognise as true.

Susan Clark

Gazing

Gazing, into this small window of time,
I see stories unfold on crisp pages,
I see beauty in this window of mine,
Butterflies escaping cocoon cages,
Bright eyed wings uncurl all in a flutter,
on the branch of the tree with the green leaf
Browning, drifting, crinkling, joining clutter.
Dear window, in mind's eye, such a brief
journey, to glimpse a faraway place
I know not when I shall see once again,
or feel the cold pinch, the hot slither lace
down to the fingers, wrapped around a pen;

> In need I am of the window I see,
> That gathers dust and is locked with a key.

Bilal Saloo

Shakespeare

When Shakespeare lived and breathed upon the earth
And words like sentient spirits flew from his pen
How could he know how much his words are worth
To those who read and speak them later when
He wrote in haste? A deadline for a play
Drew words in torrents from his teeming brain.
The sonnets, for his pleasure, passed a day.
The quality of writing was not strained.
Words do not fade and flake with passing time
Or smash, like Pieta or Parthenon;
Erode, like stone, with rain and city grime;
Succumb to accident or mishap, and are gone.
These deathless words are much more than they seem:
He gave us them; we sleep; they help us dream.

Brock Theakston

Communication

How do you speak, by pen or voice?
There's always a choice.

There's nothing like the written word –
Time to think, time to inspect,
Time to delete, time to correct,
Whether by letter, email or text.
But interpretation can often be bent,
One hears the voice but not its intent,
One takes offence when none is meant –
Time to pick up the phone.

Hearing the timbre gives its clues,
The tone of voice the speaker can choose.
Better still is face to face
The tongue can deceive in countless ways,
But body language with face and hands
Can help us the better to understand.

Cecilia Wilkinson

Mind Your Manners

They say that manners maketh the man
But good manners also open doors
Can put an end to wars
It's hard to want to settle scores
When someone says they are sorry.
When they show you respect
It's hard to reject their sincerity of intent
And the need to vent and rage melts away ....dissipates
But what about online etiquette?
How do we learn the art of good 'netiquette'?
How easy is it to misinterpret the written word,
When we are text shouting just to get our voices heard.
Respectful lines of communication become increasingly blurred.
Facebook admins tested on their codes of conduct skill,
by Trolls who roam airwaves, going in hard for the thrill
of the cyber kill.
How do we stop this online vitriol often typed in upper case?
Spewed out angry words unlikely to be uttered if face to face.
Don't become an online fool
Just follow this one simple rule
If it's not ok to say it in person
Then nor is it fine
To say it online

Christine Renshaw

Fellow Travellers

They sit side by side with their hand-held devices
Patiently reading of virtues and vices,
Exploring the world with a questioning finger
Philosophy, politics, long will they linger
They speak to each other and share their conclusions
Discounting the myths and dispelling illusions.
Comparing statistics or searching for clues.
Assessing investments or reading the news.
They glance at each other on leaving the train,
Then walk away, lost in the screen world again.

Freda Davis

Zero

So you're positive you're negative.

But not in a negative way
in fact you're being quite positive
about being negative,
I think that is a positive attitude.

But the real test will come
if you are positive about a positive
and not automatically negative
about a positive, which is
what everyone will expect.

If everyone expects something
and you comply that could
be seen as a positive even if
it is a positive about something
of which you feel negative.

So if a negative is positive
and a positive is negative
and negatives and positives
cancel each other out

does that mean absolute Zero?
which is very chilly at Minus 273°C
which is as negative as you can get.

Ian Jones

Positive Opposites

If I was the sun and you were the moon
We would be together in morning and noon
If I was the blood you would be the skin
We would never be in sin
If I was hot and you was cold
We would stand together brave and bold
If you was the morning and I was the night
We would never ever have a fight
If I was curly and you were straight
You would always be my mate
In this land where blue bells jingle
and poppies pop
This would be a land of friendship and kindness
With piles of smiles on everybody's face
In the land of love

Alexa Grace Friedl-Hirst
aged 8 years

Belonging in the Pennines

You are the waltz moves and the feet.
You are the metronomic beat.
You are the ferns, you are the gorse.
You are the wind upon the moors.

You are water in the fountain.
You are the paths up the mountain.
You are the mist as it rises.
You are fun-fair and its prizes.

You are the nimble candlelight.
You are the heron taking flight.
You are the rhythm and the rhyme.
You are the drummer beating time.

You are the daily towpath grind.
You are the focus and the mind.
You are the rainbows and the skies.
You are all of these Goodbyes.

Sarah L Dixon

Yorkshire Love Poem

This little rhyme is about me and you
in a landscape that's uncharted and rough
like the brave monocled explorer who

attempts to tackle the prettiest clough
and meanders when they're away from home
until of drifting they have had enough.

From the abyss I survived on my own,
I cherished each moment I felt carefree
whilst tracing the borders I had outgrown.

We can enjoy the view from the valley
as we write together our best tales but
even biros run out eventually.

There are other peaks that I could pursue
I suppose for now you will have to do.

Sarah Boniface

Diary of an Industrial Landscape Artist

Creating canvases can
Cause a cavernous chasmic conundrum
Considering
Quarrelsome. Questions.

Consulting critique can just
Cocoon copious concepts crying out
With courage
A concept; a change

Conveying a cosy scene
Charming, cute Chapels and choked chimney stacks
Coupled up
Mellifluously

Brushstrokes motion mind moulding
Harmony hues hum harmful histories
Moorland tales
Humble harsh homesteads

Hanging on in heightened hope
Synergy restored. Final work dated
Neatly signed
Miss James. Elated.

Ashley Cundall

Pack Horse Trail

They could have been laid down by the Romans,
These squarish stones embedded in the earth.
Like a spinal cord they snake over hills
Humanising the silent dark peat and grass.
Many first took root in the medieval world
Serving the monastery and the manor.
Three centuries ago they were the trade routes
Over the wind-swept unforgiving hills.
Even now, clad in rich hiker's fashion
The rain can turn you into a bedraggled
Stumbling thing and the snow can blind you
As your senses mingle the earth and sky.
I try to imagine the pack horses
Loaded with goods and driven by men
As I walk the trails above Todmorden.
The horses come to mind so easily,
But the men belong to a different
Mental universe where not just moors
With long and winding trails are walked upon
They walked between the poles of heaven and hell.
And I walk to walk.

Keith Charlesworth

Striding Edge

High above the tarn, where buzzards soar
and ravens rasp their guttural call,
Helvellyn beats its chest and thrusts out a rib
to challenge the adventurous rambler.
Once fashioned by a glacier's freeze and thaw,
this saw-tooth ridge now endures a new assault.

Rubber cleat and aluminium trekking pole
accompany the boots of ten thousand feet.
Sharp arrises become polished
into rounded and slippery holds
that smear an inexorable line
to the once deserted summit.

Nature's muted soundtrack is drowned out
by the tap, tap, tapping of sticks
and clicking of innumerable selfies.
This army of ants never questions why it's here,
Impelled by absent advocates
and deaf to the call of the wild

Tom Lonsdale

Horseback

Horse riding in the South Pennies,
I let myself thrive in nature's Holme.

The vintage homes are
the landscape that I was searching for,
It is the home that I am always longing for,
Throughout my voyage.

In The Pennine Way on my horseback,
The heaviest rainfalls are nature's bosom,
Watering the hedgerows and wildflower meadows,
A fresh air for my horse and myself.

In the South Pennies,
I let my horse thrive in nature's home.

The landscape was what I was searching for,

An upland of uniqueness,
For my horse and I.

Alshaad Kara

Force Nine Gale

Shoulders of wind broadside
set a lone caravan on the move.
It rocks from tyre to tyre
and mouths obscenities
with loosened beak-like flap.
Hobnailed gusts boot
greenhouses to next door's plot
arbitrarily delivered, self-assembly
and bins are all ransacked for bags
flung skyward in a glut
of flicks and twists
to decorate hedge and field with filth.
Fingers of air pick, pick at slates
to rip off rooves as easily
as we lift 'pull to open' tabs.

This passion in such a mellow place
excites the blood
sets muscle against bone
to push against the force.
Across the field
a man walks holding flints
and greets me through four thousand years.
He on the way to his stone chambered tomb.
I on the way to mine.

Christine Hyde

On Losing Waldo

To part, to lose, is not an instant thing.
There is no moment when the switch is turned.
The past and present mingle, memories cling.
It is a process; absence must be learned.

Habits lose their fullness, are diminished;
Routines become slimmer, must be pruned:
Another presence gone, a sharing finished;
The instrument shifts key, must be re-tuned.

A corner's turned, a lonelier road ahead,
But there's no going back, no turning round.
Only one of many dreams is dead;
Believe there will be others to be found.

The head acknowledges the jolt of change;
The heart's slow to regrow and rearrange.

Brian Tilde

Waldo was a German Shepherd cross Golden Retriever dog.

Marsden Village Life (and all that Jazz)

Chill jazzy streams trickle down from Eastergate and Pule
Tinkling like the fast right hand of Lubomyr Melnyk
Accompanied by the brassy baaing of the street corner sheep
Freshly shorn so as to remain cool
In their leather jackets and shades
And the steady percussive thump of thirsty revellers
Marching toward the Railway or the Riverhead Tap
Poets like pickpockets plunder the crowds
Snatching words and phrases
From passing conversations and half heard lyrics
To be broken down in back street language mills
Then passed off as new
In anything from Haiku to Homerian epics
And all the hipster beard stroking generates enough electricity
To power the village for the duration of the festival
With a bit left over for the Christmas lights
Just two short months away

Simon Williams

Marsden Jazz Festival is an annual event

The Accordion Player

It's coming from round the corner
at the back end of the Co-op:
a river of heart-stopping melodies

swirling around shoppers
who try to hurry by, heads down
teetering on frosty pavements

resisting being lured from their lists
to vistas lost when their lives settled
for something safer than desire.

East European, I think. Romanian?
Slip fifty pence over a pound
to drop in his hat, before crossing to Boots,

automatic doors closing me into aisles
of Strepsils, cold remedies. But still
it pursues me, whenever the doors slide

open, so I listen outside
by the cold breadth of the river
where lost dreams could hide

beneath the lethargy of pewter trout
Passers-by clench their jaws, or stuff
their mouths with vinegared chips.

Some stop to smile and squeeze
a child's gloved hand. Some stare.

I walk towards him as the last notes fade, ask
where the music's from. 'From everywhere.'

Cora Greenhill

34

Rushbearing

Wi' t'jingle o' bells and the beat of a drum
Look up t'road, for t'Rushcart 'as coom.

Melodeon, fiddle, ribbons and clogs,
They mun't coom too close, or they'll freighten the dogs.

They start wi' a brew and a quick dance, not much,
Then pull th'eavy cart for a service i' church.

Wi' t'rushes on t'floor, and a dance in the aisle,
T'vicar says "bye, thank for mekkin' us smile"

Then t'dancers, musicians, t'cartpullers, all t'lot
Dance off t' the pub, get a beer in their pot.

A dance round t'village, an'a quick bit o' grub,
Strange how all t'cloggies end up near a pub.

Wi t' pounding o' t'clogs, an' t'figures o' t' dance,
They practice for months, an' leave nowt t'chance.

On t'day o' the Rushcart, they'st be at theer best,
Clogs polished, bells breet, an' out dance the rest.

It weren't very long sin' I danced theer mysel',
But th'owd legs gave out, put mi clogs on the shelf.

But now I'm content just t'watch,
An' remember
As I'd danced wi' t'clog de la clog
At t'village Rushcart.

Alan McKean

36

The Yorkshireman

A Yorkshireman that I was born, A northerner and proud
Not one for laughing and giggling or mixing in the crowd
And I miss the days when as a bairn, I walked up those rolling hills
I could see those sheep a bleating, I could see them rusty mills.
Those mossy-covered dry stone walls that carv'd evry field o' green
And made it look like patchwork on a quilt that's far too clean
But now those days are behind me- I've left the quiet and the pretty
I went off to find a job and landed 'ere in London city
And the place is packed with traffic and I'm sick of all noise
The exhaust fumes fill up my lungs and it's full of city boys
These fancy Southern lads dressed in their best bib and tucker
Who think they've worked it out and that I'm the stupid chuffer
But they don't know what lies up north away from the smoke and rain
That England's very paradise is just two hours on the train.
I've been down south a while now working 'ere for seven year
And I've found that these cockney lads know nowt about good beer
In Yorkshire pubs the golden ale slips down't throat like honey
In London the beer's not half as good
                              but they'll charge you thrice the money
The scran 'int much either, it's made of plastic putty
A falafel wrap's alreet for some but where's me bacon butty
There's are a million and one kebab shops
                              where you can buy a bag of chips
But not a single one with mushy peas and bits
Barber shops and nail bars, a coffee place or two
Frappuccino's by the score but not a decent brew
But every time I'm up north it changes every day
And I can't help feel that Yorkshire is a concept in decay
I think I'm out of London for greasy spoons and pubs
But London follows me up with its cocktail bars and clubs
The Yorkshire where I was moulded, the place that made up me
Those mossy-covered dry stone walls is where I long to be.

Eddy Dennis

Special Journeys

The house is riot of activity
Dad preening in the bathroom mirror, smells of Old Spice
His hair is sleek, Brylcreamed into submission
His leather shoes spit and polished within an inch of their lives
He steers his tie with precision into the perfect spot
While Mum is downstairs making sandwiches
Directing children with the well-honed skills of an Octopus

Dad manoeuvres his family of dawdling carriages
through the quiet streets
Constantly checking his pocket watch and tutting,
till we arrive at the station on time
We pass like royalty through the crowds,
escorted to our seats with the tip of a hat
Finally, collapsing into the soft carpeted chairs,
the smell of adventure in the air
As the train leaves the station,
I sit quietly waiting for my day trip mission to begin
My older sisters already arguing about some boy,
soon they will grow louder
Dad stretches out his paper
in readiness and we all disappear behind it

I watch the red brick buildings of Manchester
give way to fields of emerald green
Our carriage rocking back and forth
as mum straightens her pencil skirt
Removes her scarf, patting at the falling curls,
wriggling toes free of high heels
She is ready to relax

"Right, who wants to win an extra scoop of ice cream?"
Eager hands fly up like helium balloons,
she works the mesmerized crowd
"Then let's see who can spot the most rabbits"
and there it is the challenge
The day out has begun in earnest,
small as I am, there will be but one victor
As I press my face against the glass and start to count

Linda Downs

Marketplace

The candy-stripe canvas on the Saturday market stalls
billows in the breeze. Stripes dance dizzily – pink and blue
in the wind, anchored parachutes with desire for freedom.
Now a rogue gust jolts and shifts the trestles.
Flimsy wooden structures jerk. Crates
and high-stacked cardboard boxes tilt and slide.
Red apples tumble, roll over shiny cobbles,
silk scarves turn to limp rags on the puddled path.
A wicked wind sweeps up, puffs up plastic bags:
gaudy weather balloons launched to the cloud:

sacrificial offerings to appease
that inconvenient, bothersome breeze

Vera Marston

Underground Unaware

like the insignificant drop in an ocean
like the merest dot
like the vaguest notion
like the hint of a fleck
like the point of a pin
i am the speck which has crept within
your long-term resident guest
silently lining your lungs like soot
darkening a chimney breast
laboured breathing will be the norm
as your respiratory system I deform
inflammation, fibrosis, cavities, nodules and necrosis
will leave you with
a chronic cough shortness of breath and cyanosis
coal workers fear me as a diagnosis
why? i am yours truly
pneumoconiosis
or
when extracting your last breath - death
i am legion
I am everywhere
I am no germ seeking germ warfare
i am just
as recorded in common prayer; dust
which you inhaled
underground unaware
so ironic, so unfair

Stan Duncan

41

No fence holds him

His heavy feet ached and blistered
dry heat penetrated his bones.

He marched with his memories
and fond thoughts of love
yet excited by possibilities
and a kaleidoscope of dreams.
Tan leather enclosed his possessions
a heavy burden to sustain.
A sturdy stick laid a dotted track
wind-dragons blew their fires to erase.

As he passed, all who watched
felt awe at his stamina and progress.

If they had given time
to sit and talk awhile
their minds would have calmed
confident peace been found

A way would be lit to give them bold choice
a treasure for them, forever.

Edna Hartwell

*This man walked the Marsden roads and moors all summer 2022, then disappeared.
No-one knew who, what or why he was there, but by some strangeness everyone claimed
to have seen him no matter where they lived in the village or any of the surrounding hills.*

What's Normal?

Is it the normal, or is it the new normal?
or normal-normal or never normal.
Or nothing is never normal, or nothing is never-ever normal
or things will never be normal.
Or are there Secret Normal Groups?
      The How normal are things?
            The How normal is it?
            The How normal is normal?
And the 'How long has normal been normal for?
The wannabe norm's, the norms weathering the storms,
the I am the norm, the never was the norm,
the think they're the norm, the how's the norm?
The won't ever be the norm,
the don't upset the norm's the norm, the whole norm
and nothing but the norm,
so help the norms.
The hoping it well get back to the norm as I only live the norm
and only the norm will do.
When tomorrow comes, what do we call it today?
Do we say normal or un normal?
A dream or a nightmare, or do we just call it another normal day?

Paul Power

Beneath our feet

Snow hangs on tight to
weather weary tussocks,
ice a reality on Wessenden Head,
and your weak eye cries
false tears in permafrost
as tips of fingers worry about frost bite,
the numb edges of this landscape.

Beneath our feet
air bubbles are frozen,
diamonds in hard water.
Your smile reflects the joy
of breaking ice, the crack-crack-crack.
Somewhere hidden in igloos
a pheasant's guttural alarm
warns us of hearts, the fragility.

We both saw for miles,
the blue over white tops,
all the way to Marsden,
to the little houses,
to the constant line of cars
on the Isle of Sky road.

This is a place,
top-of-the-world, some other planet,
peat-beds-lost-forests-hidden-jewels-dead-secrets
beneath our feet.

Penny Sharman

Wild Side

There's something wild inside of me,
At night it whispers to my soul,
It tells me I should try to fly,
Perhaps that wild thing is an owl?

There's something wild inside of me,
Its colours shine within,
It oozes transformation,
Perhaps a butterfly's within?

There's something wild inside of me,
It has me pacing back and forth.
It's caged in captivity,
Perhaps a tiger is unearthed?

There's something wild inside of me,
It's raring to explore.
It's a powerful, untamed beast…
Perhaps it's just a boar.

Rachel Mulqueen

Moorland Fires

I'd scream if I could,
I've been violated again,
The searing heat spreading
Across the curves of my being.

I have numerous black scars now,
People from all over the land
Come to fight in my name,
To fight for my very existence.

But my wounds take too long to heal,
No new life can spring from me,
No doctor can medicate me,
Time is my only salvation.

I'd scream if I could,
Maybe then you'd take more care,
Take more pride in me
And all that I can offer you.

Phoenix Nixon

The River Holme

This river was wild once,
a child of the moors,
a free spirit, its channel
a home, not a prison.

When humans came here
they feared its capriciousness
tamed it with weirs
constrained it in stone.

They gave it a name
redolent of meek domesticity.
Subdued, foamed and rainbowed
with chemicals, it sang to their tune.

But listen …
in tree-hidden alcoves
the natives are plotting. Bold saplings
stride down to the river bank.

Up on the hillside the birches are marching
through recaptured fields;
in slow motion explosions
even the soil is bursting through walls.

The water is quiet
but do not be fooled
This river was wild once.
It will be so again.

Edwin Cooper

Breathing space at Blackmoorfoot

At the reservoir wind catches my breath,
hurls it with water onto the path;
surging waves have created
a larger, fiercer, darker stranger;

unlike days when the sun
strikes diamonds off its surface,
lifts the spirit,
gives breath to the soul;

a last breathing space for another,
who I only know as Rita,
some flowers on the railings,
her name written on a card.

Anne Broadbent

Bedrock

Stone slates the roofs, sloping this valley down,
stone hedges the fields' edges that rise above this town;
stone hobbles, square-cobbled, behind its church's back,
stone steps out in stiles along its rural tracks.
Stone lies stored as quarry, lies layered along these walls,
stands firm in old gate pillars, and lintels over doors.
Struck, chisel-licked, and lichened, the Pennine's stony face
stuns, surveys, surrounds us: bedrock of this place.

Susan Dornhorst

The City

7am. The beast awakes
As the pale sun breaks
And reflects in the glass.
In the maze of urban streets,
A cacophony: the whirring
Of machines and radio
Chatter. The city still
Sleeps as night becomes
day. Lost away, as its
Denizens change hands
Once again. Things always
Remain the same. A sea
Of faces without a name.
A pointless masquerade,
Where monoliths, like giants,
Appear to dwarf the sky. And
Shapes skulk about in them
Shade - already crumbling
In the powdery air...

Ben Gardner

The Beauty of Community

A knock on a front door: "Just came to check all is OK?"
"We've noticed that we haven't seen you out these last few days."
A group of shrill young voices, children playing in the street,
Their joy at running freely shared with all those that they meet.

A recipe explained as neighbours chat over a fence,
"Ingredients from market tend to cost a few less pence!"
A dog without a collar walked back home after escape,
The sound of a loud argument that goes on 'til quite late.

Two pensioners on sticks trying to put the world to rights,
A group of teenagers hang out as day turns into night,
A meeting held to organise a charity event,
Opinions differing on where the raised funds should be sent.

A family stops to coo over a baby with a mother,
The conversation flowing like they've always known each other,
A grumpy shout echoes after two quick, mischievous youths,
Their rucksacks freeing apples that fall down around their shoes.

A woman clad in dressing gown jogs down a garden path,
Then runs to her friend's house with some news to make them laugh.
A phone distracts a man who almost walks past an old mate,
They stop, shake hands and catch up leaning on a rusty gate.

A wave to say hello, a hug and smile upon a loss,
Compassion, thought and care all offered up without a cost.
So many similar happenings in all communities,
As simple daily life plays such a precious part in these.

Claire Culliford

I dare you

We, each and all have a voice,
Whether it's heard is often our choice,
Remember in words there is healing and power,
Expression can allow us to flower,
So go on and let yourself be heard,
You will find that to share shows the value of word,
I know, I concede that talking can be scary,
And who we choose to do it with one's allowed to be wary,
But often those close,
Those that do care,
Are delighted and blessed when we trust and we share,
Know that what you feel it has worth and has value,
And even the fears when in the light might cause mirth,
So get those dark thoughts out into the light,
And allow yourself to heal and trust in a future that's bright.

Martyn Hammonds

A shared commonality

We've all stood at a bus stop
Or a platform at the station
Dreamt with wondrous hope
Of a tearful standing ovation
We watched the slalom of a droplet
On the window of thunderous rain
Touched by elation's wave
Or the thrust of utter pain

We walked where others before
Slipped and slid in freeze
Where hats and scarves are worn
In the taste of autumnal breeze
Runners ran where loiterers live
On the corner of a street
Many steps have stepped before
Where today we find our feet

It is commonality that lives and breathes
In every day's mundane task
Standing in the bus or train
And smiling behind the mask
The friend we have not yet spoken to
Though passed so many times
Community's shared togetherness
In the sweetness of a rhyme.

Mohamed Saloo

More in Common

Here in Batley and Spen we've a diverse community
Regardless of race, religion or background you get no immunity
From overcoming the problem as part of the solution
As we all join as one in our home's evolution
As our very own Jo said, we've far More in Common
Some want to divide us but united we'll stop 'em
At the Run For Jo we'll all be together
Whether walking or jogging, or full hell for leather
At the Great Get Together, we'll share lunch and dinner
And so much tea and cake you'll be much less thinner
Batley, Birstall, Heckmondwike, Cleckheaton
And all over Spen, you'll see our spirit unbeaten
With unbreakable Yorkshire spirit and heart
Our love of God's Own Country, sport, and the arts
A fresh brew to drink, and good food to eat
We know that when we're together, it'll "be reet".

Graeme Rayner

"*We are far more united and have far more in common than that's which divides us.*"
Jo Cox MP, her First Speech to Parliament, 3rd June 2015

Jo Cox MP was murdered in 2016. After her death, inspired by her message of unity, twice a year "The Great Get Together" encourages people to make new connections.

Like Sheep?

In Marsden
there are people and sheep;
people who like sheep and people
who dislike sheep. People who like sheep
dislike people who dislike sheep and people
who dislike sheep dislike people who like sheep.
The people who like people who dislike sheep tell people
who dislike people who like sheep to go and live somewhere else,
where there are more people who dislike people who like sheep and people
who like people who like sheep tell people who dislike people who dislike sheep
to go and live somewhere else, where there are more people who dislike people who dislike sheep…

It's getting fraught, turning rank.
Facebook is on fire.
Last night there were fights in the street about sheep

58

But if people who like sheep
could learn to love people who dislike sheep
just a tiny little bit more every day
and people who dislike sheep
could learn to hate people who like sheep
just a tiny bit less
then after a while
the whole fracas
would simply
fade
aw...

Alan Stanley Prout

Friendship

My friend brings me sweet things
And wine
She sits by my side.
Hears my sorrow, feels my joy
Confidante, confessor, healer and guide.
Together we weave a shawl
To cloak in times of need.
The weft of hugs
The warp of talk
The borders of acceptance
The fringe of possibilities ...

Susan Cossey

Life: A Sentence

Recently
I got a text from a young man with MS,
confronting his fate from the oubliette
of a sterile sick bed.
He said, "I am squatting in the ruins of my life."

The metaphor, so stark, shocked me, and brought me to my knees.
Truly this is the heart, the essence of grief.
All phrases such as 'might there be…'
or "maybe you could…" gagged in my throat.
I had to recognise a stark and terrible truth:
There are no happy endings. None.
This man was 'In mourning for his life',
his health, his youth. All his possibilities.

I hold out my hand, but he is too weak to take it,
too far into his grief to lift his eyes to meet mine.
And I am too shallow, too light-footed in life,
to go that journey halfway with him into that cruel disease.
So I am forced in some alien way,
to be the one
standing looking down at the man in the oubliette,
having no rope to throw…
Just feeling that inexplicable curtain that falls invisibly, palpably,
between the well and the unwell…
and the terrible sadness of that.

Mary Lister

The Last Time

There's a last time…
A last time you see someone;
A last time you smile and they smile back;
A last time you hug;
A last time you kiss;
A last time you speak.
You never know it's the last time,
Until there isn't another time;
Then you wish for the last time again.

Jane Griffin

The Role of Ramadan

Violent harangues of hunger pangs,
Solemnly suppressed by invoking hands.

Tired, listless, lethargic limbs,
Silently cleanse the soul from sins.

Somnolent, tired eyes,
Stay awake to seek their prize.

Dehydrated, throbbing heads,
Understand the blessings of health.

A gathering of pleading tears,
Release their inmost guarded fears.

A month of abstinence leads to thankfulness.
Spiritual maintenance.

Sahera Patel

Where do you go to?

Perhaps it takes you somewhere safe;
a special place. In those moments,
those seconds, that it steals.

Perhaps the nothingness grasps you in her arms,
cradles you 'til the storm has passed.

Perhaps you're saved amongst angels,
and rainbows, a safe place,
spared from the turmoil and
wreckage of mind and body,
just for a fleeting passage in time.

Perhaps your beauty is restored;
like that of a rose after spring rain,
revitalised and born again to bloom.

Sonia Zoref

Collateral Damage

Oh to have a complete house
That stands with roof and floor and all
See happy faces in the warmth
No glass, no dust; a solid wall.

To see a clock whose time is now
Not frozen when the bombs came down
A table and the kitchen chairs
Not ripped and tipped and burning brown.

I could be helping kids at play
And work, and cook, and smile once more -
Not fixing up the shelf again
Or putting planks across the door.

We could find quiet again at night
All dreaming safely in our beds;
No screaming sirens, flames or shells
That shake our teeth and shake our heads.

Oh, but I'm tired of cold and dark
And roads where mangled buildings sigh
I'm tired of crying, pain and hurt
And bloodstains where the lonely die.

So I am praying to some on high
To save us, help us, end this way
Of barely living, scratching life
From craters – just a normal day.

Henry Curry

Chief Executive

How brave, how strong he is, they said,
unswayed by sentiment, never scared
to take the hard decisions.
And when I saw the carnage that he left
– careers ended with a word,
communities gutted and left to die –
I too could only marvel how he
steeled himself against such pain.

But as I came to know him, I could see
he has no need to do so.
Each round of cuts, each sacking
leaves no mark on him, except a
little smile of satisfaction,
having trimmed the bottom line.
He feels no pain that's not his own,
knows no value that is not for him.

He lacks a sense most of us have.
I might feel sorry for him, but
he is fortunate in his deficiency:
others must fight to bend the world
around their disabilities.
His lets him blunder round it unperturbed:
a blind, deaf man, driving his bulldozer
through crowds of screaming people.

Tim Taylor

Play up, play up and play the game

(With apologies to Henry Newbolt)

At school it starts, all very tame,
Building men who think the same,
That they deserve the world's acclaim
Play up, play up and play the game

Their golden lives go on to fame
Blessed by contacts, blessed by name,
Power or wealth – or both – their aim
Play up, play up and play the game

Setbacks only fan the flame
There's always someone else to blame
Call me Sir (or, rarely, Dame)
Play up, play up and play the game

For others, poor or sick or lame
Who childhood horrors overcame,
"Don't work hard enough" they claim
Play up, play up and play the game

These brazen men show little shame
For this world they casually maim;
They stand together and exclaim
Play up, play up and play the game

Tansy Hepton

The Fool, the Prince, and the Wise Man

Follow me said the Fool,
I will lead you wherever I may go.
Allow me, said the Jester,
To take you to the Promised Land;
Where silence is not wisdom,
Where thought is not reason,
Where truth is what it needs to be,
According to the season.

Listen to me said the Prince,
The way is mine, and mine to know;
Take my hand said the Statesman,
And I will show you the Promised Land;
Where fire is just a flame,
A promise just a vote,
Passion just a hollow name,
And trust a threadbare coat.

Consider me, said the Wise Man,
Take doubt as your keenest guide.
Imagine, said the Prophet,
Your dream of the Promised Land;
Where fear will not destroy,
Where justice is not lost,
Where hope will never stumble,
And freedom has no cost.

Peter Rudman

Heartache

Pains in the chest that woke me up at half three,
Ambulance to A & E isn't where I want to be.
Trolley in a corridor,
Waiting for a doctor,
Nurses busy running round tryin' to get the queues down,
Shiver while I'm waiting in a split right down the back gown.

Lying in the heart ward, wired up like a switchboard,
Watch the nurses passing, looking at their clipboard.
Tell me what the tests show,
Don't you think I should know?
Couldn't get to sleep cos all the other guys were snoring,
Blankets thin and twisted, mattress hard as boarding.

Waiting for the staff-nurse, waiting for the x-ray,
Waiting till tomorrow till I find out what the Docs say;
Lying here in limbo,
Still be here at Chrimbo,
Dinner unappealing, staring at the ceiling,
Wait for people stopping by to ask me how I'm feeling.

Consultant on the ward round, patients getting nervous,
Coming out with words like endocrine and epidermis.
Baffling the layman,
Holding court with housemen,
Scribble down instructions, detailing the ailment,
Prescribing medication, specifying treatment.

Tell me what the dose is, tell me the prognosis,
Atherosclerosis or a coronary thrombosis?
Do I need a surgeon,
Or cardioversion?
Give it to me straight Doc, don't wrap it up in jargon,
Give me ten more years, and I'll think I got a bargain.

Trevor Alexander

Lamb at a Crossroads

A little lamb bleated
in the middle of a road
far from the fields
and the flock that it followed.

From the vegan café
staff left cups of char
to lead the little lamb
away from the cars.

With a couple more cries
the lamb climbed the pavement,
now wafted by aprons
and barista impatience.

While further uphill,
a shepherd stood beside
a shaky old gate,
waving as a guide.

The lamb hurried up
to the shepherd and beyond
and the vegans tutted,
went downhill and were gone.

Owen Townend

Bright Thing

I'm drawing imaginary dragons or monsters
in the back room of the terraced house on Grange
when my father walks in and takes the pencil from my hand.

He sketches an aeroplane for no reason other than to show
me he can; his party trick. The roughness of his skin; the oil
and coolant ingrained that scratches against ink.

My mother steps in and outlines the shape of an elephant
floating in space, oblivious to all the things that surround it.
Later I throw paint at it all, bring the monster to life.

David Coldwell

Anniversaries

They come and go, year on year
They are meant for love and hope
That all depends on what they are for
They can be sweet and also sour
Happy and also sometimes sad
But no matter what they always come
They bring up deep feelings for us all
About what life is about right now
These are moments in time to remember
So, no matter what they will come to us
To show us that we are loved now and forever
So, enjoy these anniversaries as they come and go
Year on year as they are there just for us

Jennifer Smith Wignall

Missed Appointment

Recycling bin's due out. I've checked the date.
But when I reach the corner where it's stored,
A sparkling web is stretched from bin to gate.
A quiet spider guards his fragile hoard.
Arthritic neighbour, wheezing, urges calm,
Says "Hit it with that brush – I'll just stand here."
He moves ten feet away in his alarm
And shields himself behind his bin in fear.
I say, "Let's leave my bin – it's not full yet"
And help him put his bin out on the street.
We chat, and watch the spider in his net,
His home, his life, his universe complete.
My neighbour starts to go, then turns to say,
"We should be careful what we throw away".

Judith Greenwood

The Agony

Furies fuelled by solitary feelings.
Terrors, monsters, horrifying ravings
as the merciless eyes of dolls and cool-cats
*** watched a little black pilgrim whose fervours drove him mad.

Mutilating memories,
unfinished stories;
the pain of a little boy spurned
as the shame of his brown skin burned.

Soundless screams for the absence of caring
*** The agony, the agony.
Boundless dreams of a goddess to save him.
The agony, the agony, the agony.

From japes and immature jollity
to dark nightmarish imagery;
a cartoon existence of remorseless reality.
Blindfolded partners, books of wonders
all devoured, just as one does…

…Still lacerating memories,
unfinished stories;
the pain of a helpless child,
the pain of his self-reviled.

The world heard not the chaos
at the hub of his mentality.
In the black yard of humiliation,
degradation and atrocities.
So deep is the sleep of experience
where the monsters were produced;
The flowering of rage
in the white man's house.

Soundless screams for an absent mother
The agony, the agony.
Boundless dreams for something other
than the agony,
the agony,
the agony.

Pete Akinwunmi

We bought you like fish…
by the pound

Centuries of shame
crush us,
press on our history
like a tumour.
Your blood in our river
streams on
for all time,
leaves us drenched
with the taint
and guilts us black
to our
pure white souls.

John Francis

Grant me a Cat Day

Grant me a cats' day,
a day without effort or views
A placid subdued day, no work and no news
With the moggy in my lap, purring, a snooze
A day to do nothing, just as we choose.
A day of undisturbed doziness with my feline friend
a day when nothing much happens from
beginning to end
beyond sipping my tea and playing the remote
listening to blues and for the elusive blue note.

Give me a day of stroking the cat
so delightfully cushy and warm in my lap
The occasional meow, a stretch and re-curl
No worries about the state of the world.
Give me my cat and a pint of beer
as I watch the clock, read and recall my career.
A day with no comment, save on the passing of time
Cat and me watching snatches
of old 6 Nations matches
Wales winning grand slams and me sipping wine.

While cat lazes and gazes and stirs just to move
I want a 'spare me your opinion' day
because I'm in the drowse groove
a territorial dominion day
Where nothing at all happens
just these moments together
as soft as a feather
for me and my cat, Fanny Adams.

Sylvanus Olatunde Silvester

Cat

You roamed far from me
your tooth and claw absence
tortured.

By my side your warmth,
silk fur and whiskers
soothed.

Razor intelligence here
and there
surprised.

Your heavyweight crush
compressing my chest
suffocates.

Your importance astounds
my love overwhelms
CAT.

Teresa Roberts

The Jigsaw of Life

Butchers and Bakers, Soldiers and Sailors
And Teachers who work in the schools
Brickies and Joiners and Construction workers
Who work with their hands and tools
Nurses and Doctors and NHS carers
That all help to make us feel better
Typists and Clerks and Post office workers
To make sure we get that letter
Workers on an Auto production line
Putting together another man's design
Each one fitting a different part
All as important to the completed car
Authors and Writers of stories and poems
Bus and Train Drivers get us where we're going
Policemen and Firemen and Coastguard Patrols
Priests, Nuns and Rabbis that save our Souls
Artists and Sculptors and Painters of pictures
Musicians and Singers and Church bell ringers
Vets that take care of our animals and pets
Fishermen sail the seas and cast their nets
Everyone has their part to play
In the jigsaw of life that we see every day
All individuals and sometimes unique
But without one another we're just not complete
So if you go it alone and you find it's a struggle
Remember, you're a piece of life's Jigsaw Puzzle.

Roy Page

Solace

Aggression and spite hit hard,
cruel words pierced,
probing and pricking.
Too sensitive
"Sorry"
She sidled away,
left the main street
for a parallel alley,
oblivious to
surroundings,
expanding the distance,
heart thudding, tears close,
'untrue', 'unfair'
Whirled through her brain.

Percolating through the tumult –
awareness –
ahead in the darkness,
light, voices, music.
She entered.
Enveloped by warmth and friendliness,
fear subsided.
The pulsing of a soft guitar
vanquished the pulsing of her nerves.

Anne Rothwell

Diva

Perched on a high red stool
tight red dress slashed to thigh
sharp stilettos ended slender legs
her arched-back pose grabbed them.
The languid drawl of dark-night jazz
the thickening haze of illegal smoke
black moustaches lurked along the wall
no-one knew what would happen.
A surprise performance, her husky voice
audience enthralled by sweetness
the drum-beat rhythm matched their hearts
beer glasses sprawled across tables.
Her pensive song sent ripples and crack
the vivid dreams it engraved
the question hovered: was she a star?
a famous name unrecognised.
But no-one noticed her tears
no insight to her pain
the deepest loneliness here in the crowd
a lion without its tribe.

Kathy Trout

Saying it out loud will make it true

You find the note on the bedroom floor,
folded into a tiny secret,
love and lust dancing
their tango on a slip of paper
no bigger than your palm.
You stare at a blonde square
of evening light reflected on the wall,
watch it fade as the sun dips,
as you listen to the call
of your unsteady heart.

When you walk into the kitchen,
your choice made,
holding her love note like a grenade,
he turns towards you,
face composed to hide the lies,
holds up his car keys, smiles,
says he's meeting a friend from work.
You want to speak,
but simply kiss his cheek
and close the door behind him,
because saying it out loud will make it true.

Amanda Huggins

Fences

I saw my freedom through a lens of beautiful red glass.
I looked and I opined that it was my strength of will, pride
Never let me forget. Then you came along, I was saddened
To hear you speak of my failure.
You who should have loved me,
You who should have cared.

As I realised there was no love in your voice,
No love in your heart as you erected those rails.
I painted the bars, to hide them from view,
It failed as you told me I had failed you.
I grew the pain in my heart, nurtured it every day,
Till I felt it was gone, but no, that was you.

It's a dull winter day, outside the rain is falling
Once I thought life could only be good, but now
As I realise that all things fail, nothing feels new.
I call out to the empty rooms, they are silent,
Awaiting the night when you come,
All of those fences to renew.

Brian Allenby

No Documents

Tongue- tied he arrives – no documents.
Hands fisted tight, feet curled, neck stretched.
He falls into the space comprehending nothing.
Grasps nothing of what his screwed-up eyes register.
Recalls nothing of his life before this.
The shouting deafens him now, maybe forever.

Despite this he has no comprehension of where is now.
Makes no sense of what he has been through.
Where he has been all this long time.
Unacquainted with bright light, the offence on his senses,
[for he had been accustomed to dimness over months],
the shock of such discredited arrival forces him to gasp,
inhale an alien odour, cold and searing.
It pierces his unsuspecting lungs
and a cry bubbles wetly from his lips.

Heaped upon him in this instant
are numbers, names, data unending
- and documents.

This is the moment he is born

Jan Huntley

Baby Boy

How you mimic
You sit there trying to brush your hair,
brush upside down and back to front.

Oh, what a stunt
When you wave with your hands,
brumming with your lips.

How you smile
As I pass back the toy you
gave me so tentatively.
As I cook, the kitchen utensils you stack.

How you laugh
As you stand up tall in the high chair
or grab the laptop of a stranger

And as I throw you up in the air
and pretend to drop you,
you are sure there is no danger.

Stephanie Hay

A Toddler's View of Hospital

Why aren't the folk at hospital all smiley-happy-jolly?
They've got here in a Nee-Naw and been wheeled round on a trolley
It's such a big exciting place, I come here with my Mum
If I got to ride a wheelchair, I would whistle, sing or hum

But some did say "Oh, isn't she cute"
And others said "Isn't she funny"
I'm in wellies and a rainproof suit
A two-year-old little pink Bunny

Bob Cartwright

13

I am talking to a friend from school across the miles and over
t'internet
Dis connect
We feel
Connection

'Cross years
time and space
Left decades ago
In a bedroom playing Subbuteo
'Those were the best of times
If only we had known…'
I am 13 again…
I Know…

Phil Hardwick

Autistic Girl

In a lonely world, this autistic girl
is a high functioning special one,
where others play quite differently
she sings her unique song.

She's anxious of surprises,
and nervous of new food,
she worries about breaking rules,
is often in low mood.

She desires to be liked
mimics how other kids talk,
watches closely how's they play
and copies how they walk.

She invests a lot of time
in imaginary friends,
she knows they are invisible,
at eight she still pretends.

Those constant, trusted companions,
only she can understand,
with safe and loving support
they stay and hold her hand.

Her toys are displayed all neat
and stored in each specific box,
she colour coordinates her clothes
and always wears matching socks.

She's highly sensitive to smell
and only eats bland meals,
loud environments overwhelm
affecting how she feels.

She loves to read, becoming lost in pages,
with no perception of time.
travels in her own universe
absent of tick and chime.

She's rather quiet, placid and shy,
She wouldn't tolerate mean behaviour
or turn a blind eye.

She's helpful and inclusive
so thoughtful and kind,
she struggles to comprehend
a cruel or bullying mind.

She has horrific nightmares
believing everything she hears,
fighting negative thoughts
and dealing with irrational fears.

She spends all day masking,
pretending that she's fine,
until she's back with family
where she can rant any time.

She will burst in to frustrated tears
exhausted from acting "normal"
If only she knew how much she's achieved,
this little autistic girl.

Becca Hirst

Yorkshire Community

The people of Yorkshire, proud and strong
With a spirit that lasts for so long
A community with roots deep in the land
Where the past and present both hold a hand

The moors and dales, their heritage
With a rich history, they won't erase
From the rolling hills to the bustling town
Yorkshire folk always wear their crown

With a warm and friendly smile, they greet
Their hospitality, truly a treat
A love of life, with a touch of wit
In Yorkshire, you can't help but fit

From Leeds to Sheffield, they stand as one
With a sense of pride that's never gone
In the heart of England, they hold their own
The people of Yorkshire truly known

This poem was generated using Artificial Intelligence through the app named Chat GPT.
We input into the app a request for a poem with the title Yorkshire Community and this
is the result.

Huddersfield 2022

Outside the bus station no-one wants
free Covid tests anymore.
Through a fug of smoke pedestrians
ignore the fired-up preacher
more studiously than they did before.

You can barely see his face but can glean its gnarl,
incisions, incursions. He carries a snow shovel
through the town like a hod.
Its bright orange head renders it harmless.

He marches down the precinct,
on his way to sign a peace pact
with the rest of humanity.
They may not be ready for détente yet.
He invades the space of the Johnny Cash crooner,
elongating vowels with the best of 'em.

Neil Clarkson

Irish Dance Through Huddersfield

From the age of five I've felt alive
on the Irish Dance floor, I thrived.
I flew through the air burning bright
unfailingly giving all my might
practising with passion for Irish World Title.

In this small town, no one came close
It's that time of year, a new resolution
To win a world title in memory of mum
That tiny tenacious woman from County Kildare

Practising until my feet were all bare
to dance at the INEC Killarney
More chances of kissing the Blarney

Poised with passion and purpose I dance Planxty D
Feet faster than Tyson Fury
The results 500 a perfect full panel score
And finally it's been done "By yer Huddersfield one"

But that's not all, there's more to come.

Rebecca Kane

The Baker

When I was a lad and old Shep was, well, old
My mum made me butties with bread baker sold
It was warm white and crusty as fresh as can be
The main reason being my dad baked it me

He worked in Brooks bakers near the top of peel street
My mother my brother and me would go meet
In the days of no plastic or real food without that
When butter and cheese and milk was full fat

In the days before school and violence and harm
All I knew was my dad baked bread that was warm
I was sat in a shop with black tins filled with cake
There were cherries in Bakewell's my fingers would rake

Put in white paper twisted, one loaf came alone
With my father my mother and brother came home
To a small English castle in a cotton mill town
With one room and two bedrooms, stairs up and down

For the innocent child before comparisons glare
Lack of knowledge is peace
eyes never tear
Our bread was wedged in plain half's for our tea
On Monday and Tuesday Sundays meat for me

I remember it seemed happy for that moment in space
With half buttered bread Sundays leaving embrace
There's no triangular slice or cold cut out meat
Just misunderstood labour a poor man's toiled feat

Peter Jones

The Shed

Inhale the warm embrace of dark creosote.
The door swings open, creaks, closes a little.
Faint light catches a spider padding her gossamer corner.

Just enough space for one step inside.
My fingers know where to feel for the broom.
I reach out, bump the handle of a rake,
Stumble, hit the upright stump of a lump hammer.
It sways towards me in the gloom
preventing further forward movement.
Elbows angle out to balance, tip
the edge of a pile of boxes; nails or screws,
(who can tell in this dim light).
They jangle to the floor,
flat-headed and brass, fine-threaded steel,
slender and graceful
they roll and swivel on points,
then arc away to the dark recess of the unseen;
dangerous beneath my slippers.

It should have been so easy.

Ian Fletcher

Liberal Disco

Rock on to my disco
come and dance with me
the beer is really cheap
and the disco is for free.

Exercise your social skills
get a workout for your thighs
dance to tunes you used to do
remember all the highs.

When you were a young girl
let the music take you there
sing and dance and twirl around
dance without a care.

Then when the night is over
and your feet are feeling sore
you can take yourself off home
then next week dance some more.

Lay your head upon your pillow
with the music in your head
before you know you're fast asleep
tucked up in your bed.

No worries will invade your sleep
your cares you've danced away
you'll wake refreshed and ready
now, to start a brand new day.

Gill Sykes

A change of path

I'm sitting on a dry-stone wall, near a dilapidated weary stile
Do I lay in a tranquil meadow or crops of dirty lies?
One holds belief of a long-lost sanity, a custodian of my mind
The other harvests all my ghosts and a freedom I denied.

Do I reap what I have sown or farm a forgotten fell?
Retrieve a crash-landed ego, from a ladder-less murky well
I've gambled my magic beans with a shady corrupt trader
He's rebranded my subconscious, this giant will fall later

Landscapes ever changing, the canal has twists and turns
Locks stops flood and fears, while moorland always burns
The paddock gate is open, from within my secrets flee
Carpeted fields are ploughed, so stories can be free

Horse trodden tracks provide rhythm, the weirs a rush of blood
Rock formations hold freedom with trampoline conifer woods
The heather has been clustered, to construct a magic broom
I'm sweeping out the old, to walk in pastures new.

Jack Horner

The Old String Vest

I can remember as if it was yesterday,
Gran'dad wearing his old string vest.
It was quite tight across his belly,
but much slacker across his chest.
He would wear it in the hot summer,
saying how it kept him cool.
And in the cold harsh mid-winter,
it kept him warmer, as a rule.

It was always clean on a Sunday,
so he could go to morning Mass.
After Grand'ma as usual had given it,
it's weekly Friday night wash.
He'd wear it to go to the working men's club,
for his Sunday pint, a smoke and a grumble.
Just arriving home for dinner time,
before having his afternoon slumber.

He wears it to go to bed each night,
under his old and threadbare pyjamas.
And although after a good night's sleep,
he wakes up feeling fit and healthy,
a lifetime of graft and toil down the pit,
has left him far from wealthy.

So when he goes to his place of eternal rest
I'll make sure he is wearing, his old string vest.

David Honeybell

Knitting

On slender pins with pure white wool
My mother knits.
She's making clothes for babies yet to come.
Eyes still keen at ninety-three,
Experienced hands pull tight
The strands of family.
She reaches over years and seas-
Calls it her therapy,
Intends it as a legacy.
There is a tiny coat
For every grandchild's firstborn,
The pattern, feather and fan, picot edged.
Complicated, difficult and out-of-date.
Taking time and trouble; precious; intricate.
For this is not your ubiquitous 'baby-gro'.
Your everyday, throw-away, wash and go.
Your chuck it out and buy another – No
That would never do for Mother
'There's love in every stitch,' she'd say,
Adding to the tissued layers
Which lie in wait, for the day
When her journey
Finally, is travelled,
And new-born futures yet to be unravelled,
Will be linked by miles and miles
Of purls and plains, and her capacity for taking pains.

Jean Bennett

Granny Clarke

Old Granny Clarke
so straight she sits.
She knows of the dark
and still she knits.

Poor Granny Clarke,
can a camera show
how she must tremble
if her spirits are low?

For Granny Clarke
Sepia won't disguise
the sightless dark look
in those bleak staring eyes.

It is said she was blind,
though no one is sure,
that she died when a firecracker
was pushed through her door.

Yes, Granny Clarke
Stern upright and tough
after ninety-four years
she had had enough.

Chris Franklin

'Home' Smell

I love those dark stone houses,
the country smells,
the damp smell of new earth,
the possibility of snow.

Plants that look like spiders
come creeping out of garden pots,
the sound of rain on the window
when I'm in bed.

I love bath bombs in an English bath
and my granny's wild style in the morning,
scrambled eggs for breakfast
and gravy soup for lunch.

I loved England for Maudie.
she's gone and now I'm sad.
I loved the smell of her
and the way she scratched my fingers
with her tongue.

Anaïs Commère

Wire brush set

I feel indifferent to them.
In my eyes they are only
an average Chinese set, prickling
metal on cold callous materials.
I stand aloof from hearing their cool
choir by your hands every working day
whining on the fences,
so average, so unnatural.

Marta Cseh

Embroidery

I have a little tablecloth
embroidered with the sweetest touch.
Welsh ladies with their tall black hats,
daffodils and forget-me-nots.
All fashioned with tiny kisses
tenderly stitched, carefully tied.
And what fair hands were busy there,
needling, pricking, drawing thread?
Stalwart soldiers struck down
by lung disease before their time,
were locked away in wards to heal.
Their bodies needed total rest,
they must not meet their families yet.
But hands and hearts should be busy,
and what a nurse could think to do
was to bring in threads and printed cloths
so they could stitch their love and care
into those cloths to send them where
wives and girlfriends, sisters, mothers
we're waiting, longing for, their return,
if return they finally would.
I see those squaddies joking, laughing,
swopping silks and for a moment
forgetting that their lives too
were held upon a fragile thread.

Anne Steward

Epitaph for a Tourist

The spirit now is still that roamed the planet
From Nordkapp all the way to Milford Sound,
From Machu Picchu to the Isle of Thanet
Seeking something that was never found.
He searched among the fleshpots of the east;
He combed the cultured hotspots of the west.
But a dish was always missing from the feast,
And good was only better, never best.
'Find yourself,' the travel posters said:
He chased his id and ego day and night.
But truth was always just one step ahead,
Half-glimpsed, elusive, vanishing from sight.
And now the restless soul is still at last:
His future is his present and his past.

Bill Trencher

Looking for conversation

Bush hat on head in winter or sun,
shorts in the summer when he's on the run.
Dodging up driveways, opening gates,
Stopping to chat like he's one of your mates.
The friendly face on his daily round,
the trusted young man who is always around.
A reliable constant the lonely adore,
Listening out for the drop on the floor.

Where's he gone? On his hols, that would be nice,
He deserves a break, for braving the ice.
No, sadly it seems he's not coming back,
That lovely young man has been given the sack,
How can that be, what has he done?
His van was pinched by some thieving scum.
They must all forget to lock up their van,
then get caught in a chat,
cos we chat when we can.

Ian Peacock

Just Following Orders

Just following orders.
That's it.
Simply following orders.
This is not a personal decision.
Orders. Orders that cannot be denied.
There is a job to do.
There are orders to follow.
Orders are orders.
Orders cannot be disobeyed.
An order is an order.
Orders.
Nothing more.
Orders.
Just following orders.
Just following orders.

Adil Usman

Wartime Mannequin

Your sawdust leaked,
spilled like hard blood,
your moon-face smile
still stared fixed
watching nothing, nowhere.
A pale drunk distant
creature of the past
legs and arms splayed,
an irrelevant corpse.

You terrified us
with your dumb reality
waiting to snare
our childish bodies,
our panicked minds.
If we came too close
we knew you'd
spring to life and hug us with
your frightful handless arms.

You grinned, desperate but sad,
dismayed that the world
no longer needed you,
wanted no more war,
no casualties dragged broken
from bombed out buildings,
no practice bandages or
slings about your neckless head.
Repugnant, redundant, recast,
hideous.

Henry Gibson

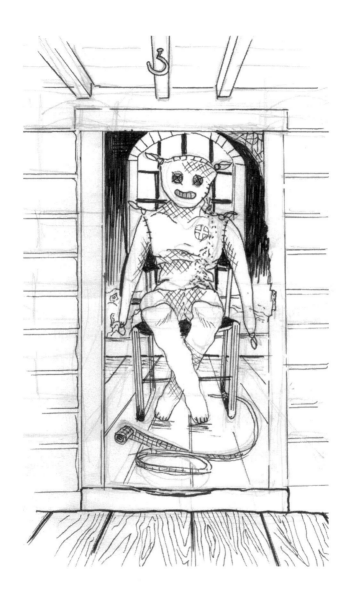

Circle of life

Arm hooked over
Hard cold wall
Carefully placing tiny
Gentle side steps

Crack, as a boy
Suddenly rushes past
Trying to break into
A glide

See how the circle has worn
Grip hard to
the frozen wall
Slowly edging forward
Fear rattled knees
Cautious hesitation
Down the long decline

Black slope of ice
Awkward brittle man
Watching the boy he was
Disappear into darkness
Dissolving
On the circle
Paralysed old rabbit
Praying he will descend
The steep death-face alive

Marc Scourfield

Getting Away with Murder

The boy sat on the floor confused
In soiled pants, cold and bruised
Force fed but too weak to stand
Scratching at the scabs on his hand
They looked like woolly red gloves
Alone, abandoned by those he loves
Easier to be forgotten
Inside feeling sad and rotten
He used to stay up on Tik Tok till late
Hang around town high fiving mates
He would score on the pitch and cheer in the rain
Until he tried to jump in front of a train
No one was coming to take him away
Solitary confinement was where he'd stay
There were no windows just stagnant air
He'd done nothing wrong, it just wasn't fair
The carers burst in loud and ready to fight
He was scared and defensive, it was the middle of the night
They pounce on him, disturbing his dreams
He kicks, spits and screams
He promised to be good, take his meds and to be quiet
He'd never been the type of boy to riot
It's the toxic environment that drives people more insane
The extra torment, bullying and blame
They removed his belongings until he could behave
But it was too late for this child lowered to his grave
The carers where not accountable
Blank paperwork and secrets hide

The coroner was none the wiser
And just jotted down "suicide"

Rebecca Friedl-Hirst

Mirror Image

I wait for my mum to return from the bathroom,
It's her fourth trip this morning,
Water tablets washing through her system:
'I can't take much more of this', she says.

The sun shimmers through lace curtains
As I notice my reflection mirrored on dad's picture,
The one on the wall next to mum's armchair,
The one which sat on his coffin.

Buxton: his last trip north.
He had just been to the tourist board,
His blue jacket bulging with leaflets
For places he would never visit.

I move slightly so that my profile
Occupies his: our noses in line
Our chins corresponding in
A silhouette of sunlight.

We have the same shape face,
The same round smile,
And for a moment, even though
I don't believe in spirits

I rest within his presence,
Protected by a love
Which reaches far
Beyond mortality.

Jacqueline Woods

Tissue Confetti

Yes, it's me who scatters the tissue confetti,
At work they call me the abominable Yeti
When I walk the corridors it is found,
That I've scattered hankies upon the ground.

And if I slip out for an illicit Snickers,
I'll tuck the blighters down my navy blue knickers.
At Christmas, at work they all clubbed together,
Bruce and Bert, Alfonse and Heather.

Gave me a present on Christmas Eve,
Some embroidered hankies, for up my sleeve.
Those cotton beauties I now keep,
Under my pillow as I sleep.

Each Friday take them with me in my check laundry bag,
Wash them with my smalls, whilst I read a women's mag.
That's where I met Gordon, bought a coffee from t'machine,
And we sat there holding hands whilst our whites came up a
dream.

So next week we're getting wed, by a vicar name of Betty,
And when we walk down the aisle, there'll be no tissue confetti.

Christine Dixon

117

Naomi

Old Naomi's thinking now about the day
On which she'd been all set to walk away
Her cases had been packed, a short note written,
And she was quite resigned to leave the kitten,
The CDs and the Kenwood Magi-mix
That she had brought from number twenty-six.
She was prepared to leave it all, to be
Free of all this, and free of Anthony.

But she hadn't gone. She'd stood there in the hall,
Bags packed and ready just to chuck it all,
But outside it had started then to rain,
And she fretted whether she'd quite catch the train
Back to her mother's, and she didn't know
Quite why she stayed there, but she didn't go,
Unpacked the bags, then, and tore up the note,
And cried a little, like a silly goat,
And thought, 'Well, Anthony is not so bad.'
Now, fifty years on, she wonders: If she had...

Old Naomi's read about the theory
That every possibility must be
Real somewhere in the quantum multiverse
When new worlds (billions better, billions worse)
Are generated with each tick of time.
So does this mean, she asks, that I'm -
Or other me's are – in some great elsewhere,
The kind of woman who got out of there?
And somewhere in that infinite Multiverse
Do other Naomi's still grimly nurse
Their dark resentment against Anthony?
While others have forgotten him and, free,
Have made of life a something wonderful,

And so have cause to never ever mull
The things they chose, or what they didn't choose
Or worry what they lost or didn't lose.
There are so many paths she could have trod...
So many many paths, but bloody God
Has fixed it so we get one single life,
And in hers somehow she has stayed a wife.

Weeks after that daft bodged departure she
Was jolted by the signs of pregnancy,
And Anthony was great and overjoyed,
And then she didn't get so damn annoyed
With him so much; he helped her keep a grip;
Together they were quite a partnership,
And when the kids came, he was a good dad;
Compared with most men, he's been not so bad,
And yes, she loves him, and well, yes, maybe
That was the reason she chose not to flee.
Or was it? Now and then her mind goes back
Accusingly; she knows there was a lack...
It was a loss of nerve, she admits quite sadly.
Yet after all, it's not turned out so badly.

George Simmers

Built to Last

I had this piece of solid comfort hand-made
Expensive, for me, in those days
When all of my possessions were hand-me-down
Its custom features
Carefully cultivated my lounge
To reflect my values
Long-lasting and hard-wearing,
It has outlived all of you.

It didn't match the fashions of the time
With their soft plump lazy
Scatter-cushion backed designs
This was proudly old-fashioned
Firm-backed and feather cushioned
In fabric where the world was leather
And brown, when only cream was refined;
Long loved, it is, by design.

Lateral G

My Hands

I remember the things that I've held in my hands
From babies to poo bags and coastal wet sands

My hands they have cared for both young and old
From cooking to bathing and the washing I fold

I've held onto teddies, handlebars and books
Then curlers and make up to change how I look

But the best thing I've held are those hands of others
Of family and friends and a couple of lovers

Whether sat at a bedside or stood at the alter
The importance of holding their hand didn't falter

And I wonder what else I will hold in my hands
As I journey through life meeting all its demands.

Cora Dawson-Shaw

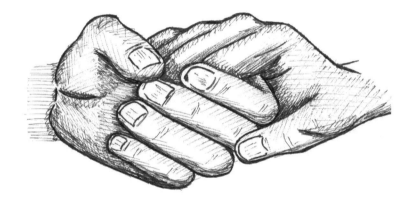

A Handbag

What *does* she keep in that handbag
which seems so big and so deep…
Is there a gun, or props for a gag
or something to help her sleep?

What does she keep in that handbag
that clinks like bottles of gin…
Something to make their tongues wag
…clean knickers for weekends of sin?

What does she keep in her handbag
that makes her stand out in a crowd?
A Gillette for her friends in drag,
that may do her Sisters so proud?

I know what she keeps in her handbag,
but I'm gagged by an oath not to tell,
not even by waving a semaphore flag…
If they knew… they'd worry like hell.

Vincent Johnson

News of Hugh's shoes

Hugh's ruse is to
canvas Sue's views
on his next pair of shoes,
not wanting to lose
her love or his muse.
They would go to peruse
footwear shops in Toulouse.
She could help him to choose
from the dozens of hues
of the shoes in Toulouse.
But she says "Please excuse.
I am tired of the queues,
I could do with a snooze,"
and an aspirin she chews.
So now Hugh's got the blues,
and whatever Sue's views
he will choose his own shoes.

John Ling

eBay

I bought it on eBay, I bought it on-line;
It was someone else's, now it is mine.
It's second hand goods, I know, it was cheap;
It was something that somebody else wouldn't keep.

It came in a box that was tattered and torn,
The edges were scuffed and the corners were worn.
It was plastered with tape and tied up with string
But the label said 'Fragile', that was the thing.

The courier left it outside by the door;
I took it inside, put it down on the floor.
I unwrapped it with care, took it out of its box;
It was padded with foam and what looked like old socks.

The seller had said that once it had slipped
And hit something hard and got slightly chipped.
It was Chinese for sure, but wasn't quite Ming,
But it looked pretty good, it looked the real thing.

I filled it with water and stuck in some flowers.
It was someone else's but now it is ours.
It didn't cost much but it looks pretty fine.
A lot cheaper than new – I bought it on-line.

Bob Trewin

Puma

Harold 'Puma' Ackroyd, swinging out fast
He and his fellow hep cats having a blast
In sky-blue slacks with thin white belt
And a fire in his eyes that can make steel melt

A wind of the waist and curl of the lip
Shaking all over he lets his backbone slip
Nobody else does it quite like him
No one keeps their tail feathers quite so trim

He's got all the moves, he struts his stuff
With the rock'n'rollin' Puma enough is never enough
He drops to his knees and lets out a scream
Before writhing on his back like a teenage dream

From Ashby-de-la-Zouch to Ashton-Under-Lyne
He has the dance halls bouncing, all the slick kids bop in time
Locarno, Astoria, The Palais and The Ritz
He whips them into frenzy, and they tear the place to bits

Everywhere he's played getting barred becomes the norm
He's got a reputation for rockin' up a storm
But Puma's got a problem that's hard to disguise
When his knees start a-knockin' he goes weak at the thighs

'Cause he's got the rockin' pneumonia, the boogie-woogie flu
And if that's not enough he's got the heebie-jeebies too
He knows very well there's more than three steps to heaven
But that he's only got one chance to make it out of Devon

He drives dark roads by night and by day he fillets fish
But he has a strong desire, one constant wish
He dreams he'll make it big, get spotted, be lucky
One day he'll sing with the King, under the blue moon of Kentucky

Malcolm J D Jones

Men with Guitars

"Men with Guitars" with Martins and Yamahas
Fenders and Crafters, it's not fame that they're after
they're only looking for somewhere to play
a lunchtime session or evening cabaret.
With plectrums and flat picks
and nifty three chord tricks
some are mean pickers others mere strummers
and a few are all fingers and thumbers.
Some folk might have already guessed
not all guitar owners are musically blessed
some need the practise to get up to par
before being accepted as "Man with Guitar"

Off into town to provide entertainment
canvas cases thrown down on the pavement
some play for pennies some play for the muse
some will sing country and some sing the blues.
Then there's Old Folky who will always depend
on those London Streets and Tambourine men
whilst an old hand from a band with thwarted ambition
plays outside a tearoom with the owners' permission.
There's a young buck, his eyes struck with stars
loves being included among "Men with Guitars".

Someone's unloading junk at The Junction
It's Open Mic night for a Charity Function
they're filling the stage with monitors and amps
with lighting provided by 80 Watt lamps.
Then in walks Jimi carrying a Strat
does anything get any heavier than that?
He postures and poses like a true guitar hero
he struggles before losing the fight with his ego
wielding his axe he plays loud and proud
and gladly laps up the whoops of the crowd.
Some men buy property and some buy fast cars
but they look on with envy at "Men with Guitars"

The sound of music comes from the basement
a familiar song with a brand new arrangement
rehearsals going well for the old troubadour
with unusual tunings I've not heard before
but then Thommo plays with a real touch of class
then Django will hit you with hot gypsy jazz
Dave's played festivals and musty club rooms
Johnny on YouTube and sometimes on Zoom
keep them supplied with real ale and spliffs
and they will regale you with rhythms and riffs
whether in flea pits or trendy wine bars
we should all celebrate "Men with Guitars"

Keith Jenkinson

Annabella Frost

the biggest fibber in our school
is Annabella Frost
she says fibbing isn't dangerous
if you keep your fingers crossed
but telling one or two a day
was getting to be a bore
and so to tell a few more lies
she started crossing more
she crossed her arms, her feet, her legs
and found to her surprise
she kept on bumping into things
because she'd crossed her eyes
her hair was in a hundred plaits
she's twisted all her toes
the dentist thought her brace had broken
when he found her teeth in bows
her mother said "it's all too much
just look what I have got
instead of Annabella Frost
I only have this knot"

Lynn Walton

Too many clothes

Why do I possess so many clothes?
I can't close the wardrobe door.
I really don't need anything else,
and yet I keep buying more.

Some of these things I don't even wear.
I've had most of them for years.
Yet the thought of having a good clear out,
nearly brings me out in tears.

Skirts and dresses, trousers and tops,
shoes and handbags galore.
Far too many jackets and coats,
and tee shirts crammed in a drawer.

I found a collection of jumpers,
some have hardly been worn,
and why am I keeping old sweatshirts,
when most are tatty and torn.

I think I need to be ruthless.
I know it's the only way.
Everything needs to be put into piles,
but I'm not going to do it today.

Susan Field

Never Ending To-Do List

I've done that task
In glory I bask
But not for long
Something else comes along

Until the to-do list is short
'What more' is my first thought
Not relief at an end in sight
I must be busy; it is only right

What else can I do?
Sometimes I feel blue
As the tasks pile high
But the end is nigh

I don't want to get to the end
Nothing to do drives me round the bend
But often doing too much can be tough
Sometimes recognise that enough is enough

Tahera Mayat

Cause of Death: Village Graveyard

Nancy Battye's end was tatty
Cyrus Boothroyd's null and void but
Betty Bottom's not forgotten.
Abraham Brier's prognosis was dire and soon
Benny Brook's life was took.
Fanny Constance fell into a trance while
Thomas Copper's flu was a whopper.
Joshua Craven's in his grave 'n'
W Edley's cough proved deadly.
Molly Gee was stung by a bee; sadly
Ellen Gelder never got elder.
Jeanne Gill was more recently killed and
Sylvia Green's no longer seen. Happily
Thomas Hey enjoyed his last day.
Connor Hutton warned he'd felt rotten but
Horace Martin's life was just startin'.
Leslie Scott felt way too hot then
Doreen Sheard disappeared but
Richard Stead is quite clearly dead. Although
Joseph Stott didn't know what he'd got
Arthur Stump had a malignant lump and as
Florence Swallow now rests in her hollow
Joseph Tweed'll no longer breed. Folk said
Joseph Varley went too early and
Alfred Weavell's killer was evil.
Vera Mear'd been feeling "bit queer" though
Derek Miller'd "never been iller". Although
Agnes Morton bravely fought on
Agnes Knight succumbed to her blight and
Thomas Neatis couldn't quite beat his.
Hedley Peckett didn't quite mek it whereas
Elsie Quirk died at work.

Chris Dance

Plain and simple please

Oh, give me back the days when I
could order without stress.
"Would you like a cup of coffee, Sir?"
 "With no confusion, yes."

"No need to state the different types,
the flavours, every bean.
A standard coffee in the cup's exactly what I mean"

"But Sir, we have the creamy ones, Americano, too –
Espresso's good for morning fog."
"I'll have a simple brew"

"There's decaf, oat milk, almond,
soy, and ones served chilled." "I see."
"And posh designs upon the froth."
"I'll have a pot of tea"

"So, would you like some herbal, fruit, Oolong,
Earl, Darjeeling?

Or maybe travel back in time,
you'll find it more appealing"

Elliot Chester

A Sting in the Tail (tale)....

Hang on the tail of a jellyfish tentacle,
See the lights from the moonbeam trail,
Run, skip, jump across the sonic waves of laughter,
Slide down the ribbon of the Aurora Borealis,
Dance, dance, dance with your lover on a solar flare,
Hold onto the arm of the Medusa Phase,
as she stuns you into submission with her embrace,
Taking you across the galaxy surfing the tides for eternity.

Dot Freeman

Dear Sparth

"Morning Sparth"
My ritual greeting, a wheedling barter –
if Sparth knows it's me,
icy fingers will not wrap around my ribs
making me gasp at the unfairness of Winter.

Yet, still we swim.

Friends wrapped closer
shivering in dawn sleet.
Even the Labradors wiggled past us
that day.

Yet still, we swam.

Through torch abandoned midnights
we're Selkies in wetsuits –
sister moon catching us,
slinking into inkiness.

When summer crowds picnic
the shores of beloved Sparth,
we skulk off to liminal Redbrook
until the changing leaves
whisper, "Return".

Jane Allighan

Cassie

Through the effervescence glow
she admires the manta rays,
and turtles swimming to 'n' fro
as gentle sea grasses sway.

A labyrinth of gold and silver,
gemstones of amethyst and jade.
Cassie begins to quiver
At this colourful brocade.

Sparkling light reflects on snaking eels,
elated, with energy and zest;
Cassie wonders what this reveals...
Gosh...a gleaming treasure chest

Fishes' scales cast a metallic sheen;
The young girl cannot believe her eyes
At this glorious aquatic scene –
For she gasps in awe and surprise

Jackie Hutchinson

Calling me softly

I want away
to walk
the waterway
to watch
the water sway
towards
the light
to hear
the water say
we missed
your walk today
so let
the waterway
unlock
the night

Simon Tindale

The Cat Watches Autumn Leaves

The cat watches the Autumn leaves
But in his heart he grieves.
For his owner has gone astray
And will never be back for many a day.

The wind is the sound of despair
For his master who is not there.
The withered leaves are not for play
As they were yesterday.

His owner has loved him nine to five
With meals to light the brightness of his eyes.
The colours play tricks with his mind
But in the house no love will he find.

No footsteps on the stair
For his master is not there.
He no longer occupies his lumpy bed
For the owner he loved is dead.

Chris Walker

Did you hear the wind?

As everyone woke up and gathered round the breakfast table
"Did you hear the wind last night was crazy"
At the school gate all that was heard was
"Did you hear the wind last night was crazy"
In the playground as children gathered to play all that was heard was
"Did you hear the wind last night was crazy"
At work everyone greeted with a
"Did you hear the wind last night was crazy"
At nightfall all I could say was
"Please don't be windy again".

Lito

Fir trees

Snow loves the trees:
they give it shape and structure
turning white nothingness
into a work of art.
It envelops gently,
shrouds their spikiness,
surrounding them
in tree-shaped haloes
till they seem no longer
wood, but trees of snow.
They acquiesce in silence:
trees are not meek
but patient, and they know
next week the rain will come.

Keith Horridge

Woodworm

Why are you so hungry
that you ate my Grandma's table?
We knew you'd been a-nibbling;
holes appearing in Mum's ladle.

My cricket bat disintegrated
and my tennis racket broke.
It quite surprises me indeed
that you never even choke.

Our piano needed tuning
when you ate the hammers for the keys.
Now the dog kennel lets the rain in
with the chilly winter breeze.

Nana's walking stick quite fell apart;
I think it's time you left.
the cat stuck in the cat flap
leaving Tiddles most bereft.

So, Mr Woodworm hear me out.
It's really not much fun;
my computer desk has just collapsed
before my homework's done.

Couldn't you possibly change your diet
and start eating up some plastic
to reduce our landfill input?
Now that .... WOULD be fantastic.

Tina Watkin

Ashes

There was no argument, when he was gone.
The Roaches: he belonged there, on that hill.
She climbed the path with me at eighty-one
to leave his remnant and respect his will.
Now older and alone, I'm coming back.
It looks the same, after eleven years
I walk that old familiar mountain track
to reunite his residue with hers.
It would be nice to think they somehow know
I'm here, stir in their other-worldly sleep.
I can't believe it. There is comfort, though
to have this place, a treasure house to keep
my memories. Mum, Dad – till I'm ashes too
this hill will be inseparable from you.

Arnold Hambleton

Rook

So handsome is he,
cloaked in black,
with eyes disguised
glass dark,
like the feathers on his back.

With a beak so sharp
for stabbing.
heavy to the point,
strong fossil bone;
never out of joint.

In the wings
there's drama ,
as feathered fingers fly
against a wicked wind,
his distant raucous cry.

His world is high
in waving trees.
He spans the waves of restless air
keeps secret what he sees.

Evie Slazenger

Six Curlews in March

Winter fading slowly this year
Stop - Start but longer days kick in
Over the village Curlews calling noisily
Searching for nesting sites in a marshy patch
A sound of the coming spring
After Winter spent on Morecambe Bay
A sea bird transforms to a moor bird
Salt marsh to peat bog and damp meadow
Gliding, calling over the grazing sheep
Pairing, landing, nesting
Checking for predators, Hawk and Stoat
Egg stealers, both
Bleached Molinia and Ling, now vulnerable to fire
Accidental or deliberate
Man's machines will soon be harvesting
Green grass in nearby meadows
Hazards facing this year's brood
Hearing the vibrating bubbling call
Six Curlews watching overhead.

Graham Ramsden

Scavenger

Growing wings wasn't the weird bit,
or when my lips calcified into a beak,
or when my toenails grew into claws.

It wasn't the weird bit learning to fly
or how well I could see.

It wasn't even the weird bit
when carrion began to smell
like sourdough bread, compost,
Wensleydale cheese.

The weird bit was falling in love—

and I was a vulture learning the vulture language of omens
(a dried-out riverbed means good luck, a blue flower
caught in your feathers means you're cursed).

I was a vulture worshipping a god of rot, vegetation, fertility;
and a god of bare earth, freshness, sterility.

It was weird laughing as a vulture;
being so happy.

Thea Ayres

Bear sap rising

The warm air an imperative
salmon called to her fat-free self.
Her snuggling whimpering fat balls,
sharply curious with tooth and claw
ready to leave the blackout den
in forests to play and fields explore.
His every sense screamed her presence
sweat-slicked anticipation drenched him
equipment honed, telescopic sights
his patience would bring its reward.
She failed to know he was there
they tumbled out of the hidden hole
trigger finger ready for the shot
a flick of the camera, competition winner.

Rhonda Welsh

Photographs

she collected images of dead things
studied their silent beauty

gone was the
shivering
twitching
darting
squirming
flapping
waving
wriggling
fidgeting

Death presented itself to her
paid homage to her fascination
piling high its perfect splendour

the last it saw
was the flash of her camera

Bernadette Barclay

The Bones of You

Your body lies
on a moorland path.
Long ears flat against your skull,
both eyes open,
staring at the clouds
as if searching for an explanation.

I stop to take a photo.
There should be tape,
like a TV crime scene.
There should be an investigation.
Some detective in a raincoat
"Only recently deceased.
Body still intact.
No signs of violence.
Cause of death unknown."

I walk the same path
mapping the seasons.
No one has bothered to move you.
Decay has set in.
For a while you were still recognisable,
but now all I can see
are the bones of you.

Sally Brown

Hope

Throughout the years, there's been wind and rain,
rattling on the windows and dripping on the pane.
Floods and disasters bringing death and destruction.
Followed by fund-raising and then reconstruction.

When I was young, the winter winds blew,
snow blocked the roads, drifting to the eaves.
There were pictures of trucks marooned at Shap,
snow-clogged sheep huddled in miserable groups.
We trudged in half-light to school, wearing wet shoes,
fighting with snowballs, making friends and fun.

But today weather comes at the top of the news.
Hurricanes and storms have their very own names,
as if this makes them less scary and intense
and to identify them in the future for simple comparison.
Now weather is explained with the words Climate Change
But is this a one-way trip to the end of the world?

Through History mankind has faced all disasters
and through them has learned to face up and adapt.
Engineers have built reservoirs to save precious water
with pipework systems to carry it to our homes.

That naughty child Pandora opened her box,
bringing fire and flood, pestilence and disease.
But the last Goddess Hope, was finally released
lifting our spirits, as well as the cloud's pall,
with encouragement, community and leadership for us all.

David Ridgway

The desolate transformed to richness

And so the seasons change.

Weather-borne hammer-blows fractured clouds,
pieces fell to snowdrops.

Tree root fingers shot earth-clad minerals
high up trunks into buds.

Magnetic fields lead the migrant flights home,
to food-rich meadows to scatter fat chicks.

Streams swelled by thaws brought natures soothing song,
fetching fish to pebble-dash their strong rich spawn.

Warm air scented by the sudden rush of flowers,
tribes of insects clattered and danced.

Skeletal cattle ravenous for sustenance
now beefed-up and bloated on ripples of thick grass.

Flat flood plains warmed by new sun sent
gentle signs of hope to those who were cold.

Everywhere the desolate transformed to richness,
once again Spring in Ukraine.

Joy Roberts

My Power

My weapon is my pen,
The paper is my shield,
My words are my power,
Something I've not really revealed.

I may not wear a tight costume or a cape,
But how my power can hit you in the chest,
In ways you didn't think it could,
Putting it in ways you understand best.

Because with this power,
I bring light onto darkness,
In ways that you could not see,
From things that have harmed us.

Arayna Tanhai

Your smile is a gift

What if we all tried for the next little while
To pause on our paths and pass along a smile
To people we see who look a bit down
Or sad or alone or are wearing a frown
Just a smile and a nod and maybe even say
'Hello' or 'How are you?' or 'Hope you have a good day'
People might not respond – might be taken aback
But maybe – just maybe – they might smile back
And be grateful for a moment to feel their mood lift
So let's give this a go – your smile is a gift

Rose Condo

COMMUNITY CUPCAKE

Above Marsden

Bus Stop

Canal Barge

Caravan

Cat in a Field

Church

Cricket

Curlews

Dustman

Fence

Icecream Van

Lollipop Lady

Man with Dog

Milkman

Plant a Tree

Postbox

Reservoir Dogs

Riding for Disabled I

Riding for Disabled II

Stoodley Pike

Widdop

POETRY IN ALPHABETICAL ORDER

AKNOWLEDGEMENTS

Like Sheep? by Alan Stanley Prout was first published in *Then become, Alan Stanley Prout,* Half Moon Books, Otley (2019).

Heartache by Trevor Alexander was first published in *Body and Soul: Poems to celebrate the 70th Anniversary of the NHS,* Whitelight Press (2018).

Bright Thing by David Coldwell was first published in *The Beekeeper's Apprentice, David Coldwell,* Maytree Press (2021).